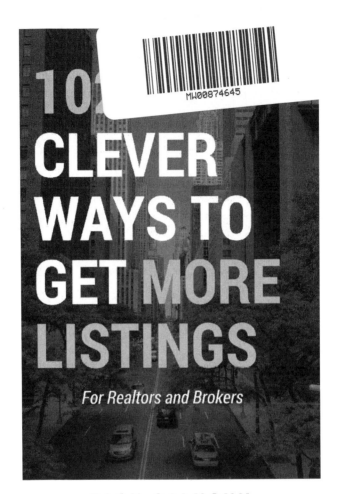

101 CLEVER WAYS TO GET MORE LISTINGS

For Realtors and Brokers

ZACH CALHOUN

102 Clever Ways To Get More Listings

For Realtors and Brokers

By: Zach Calhoun

Disclaimer

While we make every effort to ensure that we accurately represent all the products and services reviewed on this book or corresponding websites and their potential for income, it should be noted that earnings and income statements made by this book or is corresponding book or corresponding websites and its advertisers / sponsors are estimates only of what we think you can possibly earn. There is no guarantee that you will make these levels of income and you accept the risk that the earnings and income statements differ by individual.

As with any business, your results may vary, and will be based on your individual capacity, business experience, expertise, and level of desire. There are no guarantees concerning the level of success you may experience. The testimonials and examples used are exceptional results, which do not apply to the average purchaser, and are not intended to represent or guarantee that anyone will achieve the same or similar results. Each individual's success depends on his or her background, dedication, desire and motivation.

There is no assurance that examples of past earnings can be duplicated in the future. We cannot guarantee your future results and/or success. There are some unknown risks in business and on the internet that we cannot foresee which could reduce results you experience. We are not responsible for your actions.

The use of our information, products and services should be based on your own due diligence and you agree that this book and the advertisers / sponsors of the associated websites are not liable for any success or failure of your business that is directly or indirectly related to the purchase and use of our information, products and services reviewed or advertised on this book or corresponding websites.

Join our insider Real Estate community, visit
www.proREclub.com

Table of Contents

Join our insider Real Estate community, visit
www.proREclub.com

Join our insider Real Estate community, visit
www.proREclub.com

Join our insider Real Estate community, visit
www.proREclub.com

Join our insider Real Estate community, visit
www.proREclub.com

Join our insider Real Estate community, visit
www.proREclub.com

A WORD FROM ZACH

"If Opportunity Doesn't Knock, Build a Door"
-Milton Berle

If you picked up this book, you are searching for actionable ways to get leads pouring into you business. Yes, you found a list of **quick**, **hard-hitting** advice that you can implement directly into your business. When you read through this guide multiple things will happen.

Join our insider Real Estate community, visit
www.proREclub.com

1) You will be enlightened to test, try and experiment new lead channels

2) You will see examples of marketing activities that you can shape and mold (and make your own).

3) You will be inspired to believe that any level of success is possible in this business

This book is easy to read. You are handed practical and effective tips which you can apply at anytime in your career. Whether you are new to the real estate business or an experienced realtor eager for fresh ideas, you will find these 102 tips very useful.

Some questions we will answer:

- What is the right attitude to succeed as a realtor/broker?
- Do traditional marketing methods still work in the new world of social internet world?
- How can I make my website a marketing weapon to generate more leads?
- Should I outsource some of my work, and focus on winning listings?
- How can social media help my business?
- What are the new technologies I need to use?
- What simple internet marketing strategies can I use today?

How To Read This Book?

10

You can pick up this book and turn to any page. Be inspired and try the subject tactic in your business. Creative ideas and test are birthed from examples of success. You may copy some of these tips exactly, or just use the idea to create your own strategy. Either way, one marketing test can start a explosion of growth. Years from today, when you hit a wall, a rut and you need an idea to get you out? Grab this book off the shelf, pick a page and remember what it feels like to try something new.

May this guide be your inspiration.

Thanks for reading,

Zach Calhoun

Join our insider Real Estate community, visit
www.proREclub.com

MARKETING GRIT
AN ATTITUDE FOR SUCCESS

What is the right attitude to succeed as a realtor/broker/entrepreneur?

Before we get started I want to discuss a prevailing issue in the real estate agent/broker industry. The **mindset required for success.**

When you first get started, you do some quick math and you look at the financial returns for helping a client buy or sell a home. You bust out your calculator punch in the cost of hypothetical house, a 3% fee and figure you will close X number of homes a month. Then you do the math at the required investment to get started...$0. "Wow, you're telling me I can start this business with limited money and no risk? Yes I am in!"

Join our insider Real Estate community, visit
www.proREclub.com

Be careful with these thoughts...

The industry will tell you, all you spend is your time. Get licensed and hustle, and you will make truck loads of money. Easy right? **Wrong.**

The hard truth is you are in the service based business. Not a products business. This means you provide a service, and get paid for a result. With any service business comes lots of communication struggles, hard work, and **time** you spend with clients. And sometimes you waste time, lots time. So how do we move lots of listings, save time and still get paid "truck loads" of money for our effort?

You Must Think Like An **Entrepreneur**. Not A Realtor.

The key difference between big time real estate professionals that blow up their community and take over, is they think in systems (entrepreneurship) and not like a realtor. This is key to your success. And if you are just getting started, it's going to be backbone of your success. When you first start a business, you think you can do it all.... Marketing, listing prep, phone calls, paperwork. But the truth is you can't do it all. And I have good news, you dont have to, and you we will **make more money if you don't do it all.**

It is time to start thinking about your business like a system (not a realtor service). When you reach this level of thinking, you will build a system that **pumps out money**.

Join our insider Real Estate community, visit
www.proREclub.com

How Much Money Can I Make?

You need to focus on the money question. Use math to be your guide. ROI is your true north. When you are focused on investing in your real estate agency as a business, you will build a system that creates opportunity for success. Building systems make your business automatic. Create powerful direct response ads, automatic follow up, and an understanding of how to add massive value. When you create a real estate agent business (and team) you will reach the next level in your business.

We talk A LOT more about the concept of **real estate entrepreneurship** on our insider website: proreclub.com

Check it out today, and start building the mindset for success. When you get there, you will never look back.

REAL ESTATE TECHNOLOGY

Rapid advances in technology have changed how we do business. The internet allows us to quickly communicate with brokers, agents, buyers, sellers, renters and investors in property. We are no longer confined to working in an office – with tools/apps available in our mobile phones, sales transactions can be done anytime, anywhere. We are also reaching more clients from different states and countries, which widens our market reach.

With information readily available in the internet, consumers are now more knowledgeable about market trends and are in a better position to compare costs of properties. The role of broker is moving towards being an advisor, helping clients decide among the various options available.

This is an exciting age for business. There is so much to learn – to stay ahead, we need to be aware of emerging technologies and choose the best ones to grow our business.

Join our insider Real Estate community, visit
www.proREclub.com

Tip 1 - Virtual Staging

If you are trying to sell an empty house, the best way to build interest is having the rooms transformed by interior designers. Realtors usually rent furniture and decor to achieve this. This could be costly and time-consuming. But with "Virtual Staging", the design can be done virtually at minimal time and cost.

How? Using a photo, virtual staging professionals can use software to simulate a perfectly interior-designed room. So instead of showing a bare room, a potential client can "picture" the potential design of a room. No need to physically place furniture in the photo. Saving you time and money. All you need to do is send the photos and the virtual staging team takes care of the rest.

Take a look at some examples of how virtually staged properties are driving sales:

Before   After

Join our insider Real Estate community, visit
www.proREclub.com

Before After

The outputs look amazing and it is only around $40 or $55 a photo. Want to add this value addition to their service? Imagine you are talking to a potential client and they are *uncertain* about signing your listing contract. Then you slap down a portfolio example of virtual staging. Explain the process, and inform them of your ability to add this to their listing.

This will **blow away** a client and get them to sign the listing contract right then and there. Make sure you have a pen.

To get your first project started, visit
See their pricing here: whynothomes.com/order-here

whynothomes.com

Full disclosure, I own a stake in this company. So I *had* to mention it first on this list. Ok, let's get going...

Tip 2 – Personal Branding

Whenever you show a property to a potential buyer, you are also selling yourself. If you come across as knowledgeable, trustworthy and sensitive to your client's needs, there is a higher chance that you close them.

In the world of social media, you need to build your online identity before customers are convinced to meet you. How do you promote and set yourself apart? The answer - Personal Branding.

First, you need to identify your target market. There are many groups of people searching for particular properties. What's your niche? Is it the retired couple? A growing family? Recently divorced?

Second, find out more about your niche. What are their day-to-day activities? Where do they hang out, both online and offline? What are their immediate concerns? What kinds of homes would they prefer? What would push them to buy?

Third, find out how you can serve this target market. What makes you different from other realtors? From your life experiences, what combination of skills or knowledge can you contribute? What makes you unique? How would you want to be remembered by your clients?

Finally, create your Personal Brand to match this target market. Everything about you – your physical presence as well as your online persona (social media profile, blog posts, videos, tweets and comments) should all be consistent with your branding. Include testimonials from satisfied clients to build trust and credibility in your services.

Remember that building your personal brand is not a one-time activity. It is an ongoing process.

Join our insider Real Estate community, visit
www.proREclub.com

Tip 3 – People Skills

Maya Angelou said "People will forget what you said, people will forget what you did, but people will never forget how you made them feel." This is absolutely true.

In the course of meeting people in your business, whether they are home sellers, buyers, appraisers, home inspectors or co-brokers, it is still in your best interest to keep people feeling good.

Be nice. Show interest in people's concerns. Actively listen to them. Respond tactfully. Offer whatever help you can. Be patient in answering questions. Be available.

Good personal relationships are still the backbone of any business. Satisfied clients will surely spread the word and refer your services to friends and relatives.

21

Join our insider Real Estate community, visit
www.proREclub.com

Tip 4 – Resourcefulness

There will be properties available in the market very soon. So be resourceful – you can position yourself to be first in presenting your services. A typical case of 'being at the right place at the right time'.

Here are some ideas on how to find "motivated sellers":

Repossessed cars
People who default on their car payments may be in deep financial trouble; it may just be a matter of time before their houses will be offered for sale at a price below fair market value.

This information is available through banks, credit unions, resellers and auctions.

Refer to these websites for leads:
www.copart.com
www.salvageautosauction.com
http://autoreposbankowned.com
www.repofinder.com

Divorces
Majority of divorces involve property settlements. The family home becomes a sad memory and divorced couples are willing to quickly sell and move on with their lives. Make sure you have a ready list of potential buyers.

Look into court records or divorce attorneys in your area. You will need guidance on the the legal and financial implications for your client.

This is becoming a niche for realtors. The article below explains the challenges of this target market.

http://www.nytimes.com/2013/04/02/nyregion/divorce-as-a-niche-for-realty-agents.html

Vacant Property Search
You always have time to drive for dollars. Why not drive around your city looking for vacant properties? Choose those in good locations. Or those with high potential.

Call the seller, set an appointment and find out more about the vacant property. If a court case is involved, search courthouse records to get more information. These could be under divorce settlement, an inheritance – in short, motivated sellers who may be willing to dispose their properties quickly at a reasonably lower market price.

Short Sale Homes For Sale
Be on the lookout for short-sale properties. For mortgages that are 30, 60 and 90 days late, these could possibly be available on the market very soon.

Wholesaler Property Lists
Find an investor with a list of wholesale properties for quick sale.

More ideas

- An old couple who find it difficult to maintain a large home. Children are married or relocated to other cities.

- A widow/widower selling the family home to move in with their children.

- A landlord who can no longer keep up with his tenants.

- Those moving into retirement homes or hospices

- An heir who wants to dispose of inherited properties

- A sentimental homeowner on the lookout for a buyer who will guarantee meticulous care of his home

- FSBO and FRBO listings in Redx

Join our insider Real Estate community, visit
www.proREclub.com

Tip 5 – Delegate Tasks

Being a realtor means juggling multiple tasks. How does everything get done? You need to focus on sales and delegate all other tasks. Be realistic – your time is limited. Maintaining your online presence alone will take a big chunk of your time. Therefore, **start outsourcing**. Be specific about your requirements and have checkpoints to discuss progress of outputs.

Here are some tasks that you can entrust to interns, freelancers or even your own family (sharing your posts):

- Web design
- Social Media Management
- Search Engine Optimization
- Content writing
- Email marketing
- Paid advertising
- Appointment setting
- Data Entry
- Bookkeeping
- Posting ads
- Research
- Designing logo

You can help someone gain experience while freeing up time to concentrate on your business.

Some job portals are:
Fiverr.com

Join our insider Real Estate community, visit
www.proREclub.com

Upwork.com
Guru.com

Join our insider Real Estate community, visit
www.proREclub.com

Tip 6 – Face Exposure

In any business, you need to be visible to as many people as possible – both online and offline. You need to build relationships, be transparent, and show your face everywhere!

Are you shy? You can still succeed as a realtor.

Gradually take steps to expand your comfort zone. You can start with teaching your friends and family. Then progress towards organizing small meetups and bigger events like block parties.

Get inspired by Dave Crumby's article on how introverts can use their natural strengths to succeed.

http://blog.realvolve.com/why-introverts-make-great-real-estate-agents

Join our insider Real Estate community, visit
www.proREclub.com

Tip 7 - Competitor Analysis

Observe the marketing efforts of your competitors, especially those in the same city who have similar market reach as you.

Also learn from the big real estate companies. They have the budget for expensive research in their marketing campaigns. Try to do the same on a smaller scale or budget. Learn from their mistakes, and see where they double down. You can skip ahead of the learning curve if you watch what works, and just copy.

Get some ideas by visiting http://insiderealestate.com/success/brokers/. They sell their services as marketing strategists. They have agents focused entirely in getting leads through Facebook, scanning pages for prospective buyers and sellers of properties and actively responding to referrals.

Get inspired by following market leaders. Subscribe to their newsletters, follow them on twitter, become engrossed in the content of your space. Hire someone to research on the latest marketing strategies or summarize marketing books for you. You need to think like an expert to become one.

Join our insider Real Estate community, visit
www.proREclub.com

BUILDING YOUR NETWORK

Having a network of competent and trustworthy people close to your life will contribute to your success in the real estate business. Whenever you meet people, always treat this as a possible networking opportunity. Show respect, be humble and always pay it forward.

If you are familiar with the idea of "six degrees of separation", it states that people are connected in a link at a

Join our insider Real Estate community, visit
www.proREclub.com

maximum of six steps. So, the person sitting in front of you at the airport may be the "friend of a friend" of your next homebuyer.

This next section are practical tips on networking with four general groups:

☐ Complementary businesses are vendors that support your business.   You refer clients to each other.

☐ Realtor colleagues

☐ Local community. Building a strong presence in your community is very important. Not only will it widen your exposure, it will also increase your knowledge of local neighborhoods and their demographics.

☐ Social media

Remember, building partnerships has a long term ROI. At first, it cost you time and money. But in the future, leads will roll in from every angle.

Tip 8 - Moving Companies

Join our insider Real Estate community, visit
www.proREclub.com

Initiate joint ventures with moving companies. They are a great source of fresh leads. When people relocate to a new city, they may be staying in transient lodging while taking time to hunt for their ideal homes. Movers can refer your services as their realtor/broker.

In exchange, you can also recommend trusted movers to your clients, especially if they are new to the city.

Join our insider Real Estate community, visit
www.proREclub.com

Tip 9 - Termite and Pest Companies

Before finalizing a sale, homebuyers need to check the property for termites and pests, mold, water quality and others affecting the overall structure of the home.

Have joint ventures with termite and pest companies. On your website, mention your affiliation. Give positive recommendations based on your past working experiences with them. Have a list of "Approved Local Vendors."

After the sale, homebuyers will continue to work with these termite companies to maintain their property. In exchange, they should refer you to their customers.

Tip 10 – Photographers

Ads with beautiful photos never fail to attract buyers. Hire a photographer to capture the special features of a home. Also take photos of the neighborhood, city landmarks and its activities to showcase the "personality" of the area.

You can use stock photos that are free in the internet but having high-resolution photos taken by professional will definitely help your ads to stand out. They also follow techniques to enlarge a room and use apps to enliven photos. If you need specific pictures updated, touched up or brightened, I recommend whynothomes.com

Remember, great photos sell. Do not skip here.

Tip 11 – Architects and Contractors

If your client prefers to demolish and build a new home, you should have a ready list of competent architects and contractors. Choose a team that has worked with multiple projects together. It is very important that they work well together. Otherwise, there will be delays in the execution of the project.

You may encounter investors who flip houses. They will need professional architects and contractors who can help restructure a new home at minimal budget and time.

Join our insider Real Estate community, visit
www.proREclub.com

If you have potential clients who need advice on mortgage lending, refer them to a banker who can help them throughout the loan process, from application to closing. There are always new products and services provided by banks to stay competitive in the market. A mortgage banker would be more than happy to do a presentation.

Bankers can also have good sources of information on potential home sales based on car repossession, divorces, etc. This is public information but being the first to know will be an advantage.

Find a banker/friend who can keep you informed. Your future clients will need financing. So have multiple lenders you trust and can refer.

Tip 13 – Other Realtors

Get to know other realtors by attending conferences and special real estate events. These are opportunities to learn updated information of the market and new innovative strategies. Find out from fellow realtors what works (and what doesn't).

Expand your network to other geographical areas to get fresh ideas and strategies.

Maintain these new relationships by following up with informal visits, emails, exchanging blog post links, etc. Every time you add value to someone else's business, they remember you. Real estate is a referral central business. Other realtors are not your competition, they are your friends.

Join our insider Real Estate community, visit
www.proREclub.com

Tip 14 – Public Speaking

Be open to invitations to speak publicly in conferences, local seminars, fairs and events. This will build your exposure as an expert in the field. Make sure to always get photos of you speaking to a crowd. This is great for social media and marketing photos.

Have a ready list of topics that you are passionate about. Research real-life examples that you can share.

If your audience is homebuyers, discuss the following topics:

- ☐ How to avoid mistakes in buying a home
- ☐ What to look for when buying a home
- ☐ Is buying or renting better?
- ☐ What to watch out in foreclosures
- ☐ How to make an offer on a home

Events like these are opportunities to capture leads through email registration. Be ready to give out promotional materials and business cards.

Join our insider Real Estate community, visit
www.proREclub.com

Tip 15 - Local Bulletin Board Advertising

When promoting events, look for bulletin boards where your flyers and posters can be posted. The hardware, furniture shops, local spa and grocery stores are some places where your target market may be visiting.

Some important reminders:

- ☐ Get permission to post. They may require stamping prior to posting.

- ☐ Give space for the other posts

- ☐ Start posting one week before your event

- ☐ Post at eye level to get attention

- ☐ Stand out! Don't do what everyone else does. Be   creative!

Join our insider Real Estate community, visit
www.proREclub.com

Join our insider Real Estate community, visit
www.proREclub.com

Tip 16 - Have Hobbies

The real estate business can be exciting yet very stressful. Make time for your hobbies – whether it be fishing, golf, swimming, etc.

There are solitary hobbies, where you spend time alone with your thoughts. But there are hobbies where you meet people, doing things together. These are perfect networking opportunities to let others know about your business in an informal way.

Look into the following:
- ☐ Groups in Facebook, LinkedIn and Google Plus
- ☐ Local forums
- ☐ Meetups
- ☐ Do what you love, others people respect you for it

Join our insider Real Estate community, visit
www.proREclub.com

Tip 17 - Local Business Relationships

In this business, you will be working with many service providers. Maintain good business relationships. They are your source of referrals. Every client they recommend could mean business for them also.

Some examples are movers, packers, stagers, termite and pet control businesses, interior designers, furniture sellers and restoration experts, auctioneers, garage sale organizers, car sales people (see the tip on repo), government, lawyers, bankers, etc.

Once you decided to work with them on a regular basis, ask your website to be included in their reference page and do likewise.

Create a page on your web site dedicated to featuring these local businesses. Then approach that business and tell them, "Hey I added you as a trusted local vendor to my website!" Then try and leave them with material about you. You may not even need to request a referral. Sometimes, doing a good deed for a business, and asking for nothing in return, will create referrals automatically.

Tip 18 - Neighborhood Clubs

Find out all the neighborhood associations available in your city like the local Toastmasters club, advocacy associations or ethnic groups. Try attending their meetings and join them. If you are share the same aspirations about life and belief, you will make friends quickly.

These groups usually maintain a website where they post their calendar of activities, post topics of interest or give announcements. As a member of their association or a known supporter, this is your opportunity to share a link to your own blog posts. At some point, people will buy/sell/rent homes or know someone on the lookout for a realtor. With your realtor service readily available in their website, you get free advertising.

Tip 19 - Digital Tour Marketing

Open houses have been around forever. Because they work. Now you can set up a digital open house. Setting up a digital open house is a very effective strategy made possible by web technology. You basically prepare a video, walking through the property, just like you would in a real open house. You can make these house tours as detailed as needed.

This is deal for customers who prefer to walk through a house before actually visiting the place. They can be residing in a different state or country.

These videos can be posted in Youtube, Vimeo or your website itself. The exposure to the public can be very high – just make sure to use the best keywords to search your video like the exact location.

However, if you prefer videos to be more private, you can use "GoToMeeting" to set a specific time to view in real time. The advantage is that you can answer their questions at once. You can facetime with a customer on your iphone

Mikogo is another app that can be used. You share your screen and go through a video of the property while on the phone with a potential buyer. It is interactive so you can also address their questions at once.

After the presentation, you can share a link to the virtual tour for their reference or review.

Having a virtual open house is a timesaver, for both you and your potential client since there is no travelling time. The videos are also re-useable.

Join our insider Real Estate community, visit
www.proREclub.com

Tip 20 - Local Resident Interviews

Local residents are the best people who can describe how it really feels to live there. Sometimes, it just takes an interview with a local resident to convince a potential home buyer to proceed with the sale. Getting real-life comments about schools, safety and social activities can help them visualize how their lifestyle will be.

These informal interviews can be a blog in your website, a submitted article to travel or real estate sites or even an actual video.

This is a powerful way to display social proof. Sometimes, all it takes is permission and iphone video. Ask a neighbor, "What do you like about living here?" and hit record.

Here is an interview of a retiree living in Las Vegas. For those considering the move, he shares the various 'senior-friendly' activities he enjoys; then, he transitions to the affordability of homes.

https://www.youtube.com/watch?v=vo_WYuid3X8

Join our insider Real Estate community, visit
www.proREclub.com

Tip 21 - Interview School Employees

For homebuyers seeking good schools for their children, you can help them decide by interviewing the school principal and teachers. Let them share their teaching style, curriculum and school activities. If the parents have any concerns or questions, they will be more than willing to help answer.

This may seem like an extra step. A simple way to support the local school, is to post the school staff contact page on the listing. Then if a buyer wants to reach out, they have a website to contact the school.

Join our insider Real Estate community, visit
www.proREclub.com

Tip 22 – Sponsor School Activities

Parents are inherently active in the community, because kids play sports and get involved in the community. Advertise your business by being visible in their children's school/sports events. Sponsor little league teams and parent-teacher meetings by volunteering to help or sponsor food.

You can also share your realtor experiences during "career days" in schools.

Give away T-shirts or other promotional materials to keep them reminded of your business. Always be ready to spread your brand. Everyone is happy to take your card, when you buy the food.

Join our insider Real Estate community, visit
www.proREclub.com

Tip 23 - Donating to Non-Profits

Non-profit organizations also have their own websites to advance their causes. Look into organizations like breast cancer societies, autism awareness groups, alzheimer's association, disabled veteran groups and make-a-wish foundations.

Select those that you personally would want to support. Attend their meetings and ask if you can contribute posts to their website. These posts may not really be related to real-estate but in the author portion, you can add your name and your profession as realtor. Leave your website page.

Think about how you can support these communities. The more people you help, the more likely you will get natural referrals.

Join our insider Real Estate community, visit
www.proREclub.com

Tip 24 - Block Party

Your neighbors can turn into your contacts. Aside from getting to know them personally, it would be a good idea to organize a block party, with the community celebrating an event just for fun.

Common conversation topics will be about your careers, family and the concerns of your community. This is a great way to introduce yourself as a realtor and discuss topics related to maintaining, buying and selling homes. This is also a chance to learn more about their careers, and how you can mutually help each other. The person who host a great party, gets all the credit for the event. You will meet anyone who comes.

Plus parties are just plain fun.

Tip 25 – Board Membership

Being a member of your neighborhood board is a sign of public trust in your leadership. Not only will it help in the credibility of your realty business but holding a position shows that you have a compassion to serve others.

The next best thing is to be aligned with community groups and support their advocacies.

Here is an example of how a realty firm worked alongside Neighbors in Need, an organization that raises funds to help residents in need. They are promoting a membership campaign to raise more support. Betsy Butler and Karen Marcu, realtors with Berkshire Hathaway, used their wide social media presence to draw attention to the membership drive. As realtors, you can help address the immediate needs of people.

For the full story, see below.

https://edwardsvilleneighborsinneed.org/realtors-give-to-neighbors-in-need/

If there are big events in your city – like a concert or a visit from a public figure – be a volunteer. Wherever you can meet new people, these are very good networking opportunities to advertise your business.

Sometimes, volunteer opportunities will be open during calamities like hurricanes, fires or earthquakes. People turn into their best selves during such times and a bond builds between strangers. Use your communication and negotiation skills as a realtor to help coordinate during these emergencies.

Another volunteer opportunity is with Habitat for Humanity or other volunteer groups offering affordable housing in the city.

Aside from expanding your network, this will leave a positive impression on your city.

Plus, you always want to interact with folks with volunteer hearts. These folks make good clients and they have large networks to refer you.

Tip 27 - Sponsor an Event

If your city celebrates local festivals or events like 'Fire Prevention Week', 'Breast Cancer Awareness' or 'President's Day", be one of its sponsors. Although these may not be related to real estate, it is still a good opportunity to advertise your business through their flyers and other promotional materials.

Also try to learn as much as you can. During fire prevention week, for example, learn from firefighters how to protect your home from fire. This is a very good topic for a blog, something that every homeowner would be interested to know.

For 'Breast Cancer Awareness" events, learn from testimonies of breast cancer patients and survivors. This will help you empathize with clients who are facing this family illness.

From local festivals, learn more about the history behind their celebration. There could be an interesting story for your blog. Remember, engage with your prospects where their mind is already processing information. This way you already have their attention.

Join our insider Real Estate community, visit
www.proREclub.com

Tip 28 - Meetups

Meetup.com is a website which alerts people with common interests to attend an event in their city. These are great networking opportunities to meet potential clients/investors.

Meetups can be anything from a nature trip, a lecture or a fundraising event for a local charity. If you are new to this, try joining a few events. Once you are comfortable with the setup, you can initiate your own meetup on real estate topics.

If you organize an event, bring value to your meetup participants, everyone there will know who you. Remember to create a great experience, have fun and make the event about the people there, not you.

Join our insider Real Estate community, visit
www.proREclub.com

Tip 29 - Buy Breakfast

An author named Anne Herbert popularized the phrase "practice random acts of kindness and senseless acts of beauty", which she wrote on a placement in 1982. A good quality to develop as a realtor is **kindness**. This is a very competitive business but what will set you apart is your compassion for people. This translates to compassion for the needs of your clients.

So be on the lookout for opportunities to do good in the community. One example is by buying an unexpected breakfast for someone like your local firefighter, police officer or school teachers.

Breakfast will not bribe someone to use your use service. That's not the point. Breakfast is your vehicle for kindness in your community. Always be looking for ways to extend some free food.

Tip 30 - Teach A Safety Class

Homeowners are interested in topics related to safety, education and self improvement. After learning from firefighters and medical personnel, you can use this information for your blog.

You can also teach safety classes through meetup sessions, in schools and other events.

CPR may save a life. Care about the life of your community, and they will care about you.

Join our insider Real Estate community, visit
www.proREclub.com

Tip 31 - Teach an online class

Content build trust. You can use online channel to create simple instructional videos on your YouTube channel. These short minutes on camera create a powerful connection with you and you prospects.

Another way to build authority and trust is to teach through online classes.
Online courses follow a structured format and you charge the students to attend.

Some course website that you can join are:
Udemy.com
Coursera.org
360Training.com

Not only will this build your online profile your SEO reach, it will give you credibility in your market along with extra income to your name.

Join our insider Real Estate community, visit
www.proREclub.com

Many millionaires become wealthy through real estate. Perfect examples are Donald Trump and Robert Kiyosaki. Real estate courses are hot (and they may always be). So be the expert in your local community.

Build your your brand by conducting lectures on real estate. Choose a niche of real estate, where you can cite your experiences. Choose a topic like contracts or real estate marketing. Your real world experience is **extremely valuable** to young students.

If you're smart, you will find students with sincere interest in real estate, willing to learn more. You can tap into these resources to get leads or hire them part-time to manage your social media accounts. It's time to start your internship program.

Tip 33 - Garage Sales

A garage sale is a good opportunity to get leads!

While browsing through stuff for sale, meet new friends and casually ask if they are new in town. If you happen to be talking to the sellers, find out why they are selling their stuff. They may be relocating to another city and disposing stuff that they cannot transport to their new home. Their current home could still be on the market and they may be willing to sell at a reasonable price.

Other buyers in the garage sale could have recently relocated to your city and living in transient homes while searching for their permanent home.

You may also run into movers, interior designers and antique collectors who may be know of potential property buyers. Where people gather, the opportunities await.

Join our insider Real Estate community, visit
www.proREclub.com

Tip 34 – Alliance with Market Leaders

Join conferences that will build your knowledge and network. An example is "Inman Connect" where market leaders converge to share industry trends and strategies. This year's event was a gathering of CEOs from top franchises, top-producing brokers and realtors and technology entrepreneurs.

This is your chance to network up-close with market leaders. They are exposed to prime properties that have been pre-selected for their high value. This could be your opportunity to get exclusive leads from their projects and full commissions. Some might be willing to mentor you and introduce you to the world of luxury real estate.

Take a look at the link below for the valuable information shared during those four days. These are events that should not be missed.

https://www.inman.com/event/icsf17/?page=agenda

Join our insider Real Estate community, visit
www.proREclub.com

Tip 35 - Web Visitor Follow-Ups

Having a website is an absolutely necessity to build your real estate business. Whether customers find you through organic search or via search engines, your website needs to be interesting enough for people to stay and learn about you.

In your face-to-face discussions with potential buyers, what are their common questions and concerns? As their realtor, these are insights for you to create a blog post (or even as series of posts) where you can direct them for answers. Provide entertaining yet informative posts that are good enough to share in social media sites. You can also post videos or pictures of available homes.

Just make sure that with each post, there is a link to your Contacts page. Once people leave their email addresses or phone numbers, follow up! Be prompt in following up with an email, SMS message or phone call, asking how you can specifically help them in their home search. You can also include them in your newsletters and marketing campaigns.

Even if they don't respond positively at first, continue to involve them in your activities – informing them of homes that fall within their preference and inviting them to attend viewings if only to see what's available.

Don't give up – persistence will build your credibility as they get to know your business!

Join our insider Real Estate community, visit
www.proREclub.com

Tip 36 - Referrals

Experienced realtors get new clients through referrals from satisfied customers. Each referral is a compliment, proof of a job well done.

Request clients to fill up a feedback form after your transaction is completed. Ask them to assess your service – what went well and what needs improvement. This will open your eyes to your strengths and weaknesses. Thank them for their honest comments. If the feedback was positive, ask if you can use their comments as testimonial in your website.

Always follow-up with 1 to 2 phone calls or site visits after the sale so that they don't easily forget your name. Be genuinely interested in their well-being and show willingness to extend further assistance. If they are settled in their new homes, now is the time to ask for referrals.

Join our insider Real Estate community, visit
www.proREclub.com

Tip 37 – Have a contest

Using social media, you can call attention to your business by promoting a contest with prizes:

Be creative. Some examples are:

- ☐ Logo contest
- ☐ Polling on best home makeovers
- ☐ First 10 responders get 50% off
- ☐ Local trivia contests
- ☐ Questions about a city's landmarks or history
- ☐ First 5 with selfies beside your "for sale" sign
- ☐ Photography contests on local sites

Your prizes can be:

- ☐ Tickets to concerts or games
- ☐ Gift cards to local restaurants or home improvement stores
- ☐ Discounts on real estate partner services (like legal consultations, termite inspections, handyman services, home organizers)
- ☐ Electronics
- ☐ Home makeovers

Contests are opportunities to get leads through provided email addresses. It also makes it easy to follow-up with winners.

Join our insider Real Estate community, visit
www.proREclub.com

Join our insider Real Estate community, visit
www.proREclub.com

Tip 38 – Auctions

Attend auctions with new acquaintances. This is a good opportunity to assess their interest in property investments. At the same time, you will be alerted about recent foreclosures and meet serious cash buyers. Find out their what kinds of properties they are looking for. They might be interested in one of yours.

After posting a "For Sale" sign in the property, take the opportunity to walk around and meet the neighbors. Inform them of the sale – they might be interested to purchase for home expansion. Or they might know of a relative or friend who wants to live nearby. Give away one of your promotional gifts as a reminder of your business.

If they are not home, leave them a short note in their mailboxes.

Tip 40 – Befriend the Media

Reporters are always on the lookout for fresh topics. Register in HARO as a source of interesting media stories.

https://www.helpareporter.com/

Those in media are usually the first-to-know on celebrity news, property mergers and infrastructure updates. They can alert you on what's happening even before it's in the news.

Don't be afraid to shoot a cold email to local reporters. It only takes more good story for your business to explode.

Join our insider Real Estate community, visit
www.proREclub.com

Tip 41 – Prepare Your Elevator Speech

Always be prepared with your "elevator speech" or '30 second commercial".   In a few short sentences, introduce yourself, your business and how you can help others.   It usually takes only 30 seconds, the time it takes to ride in an elevator.   Practice frequently so that it sounds natural and not scripted.

https://www.thebalance.com/elevator-speech-examples-and-writing-tips-2061976

Always be ready to introduce your business - your next audience could be on the lookout for realtors.

Tip 42 – Attend Alumni Gatherings

Alumni usually gather together for reunions. These could be formal events or simple get-togethers in a home or restaurant. Since some may be flying in from different states or countries, these are very good opportunities to introduce your business and alert others about changes in the property market.

Join our insider Real Estate community, visit
www.proREclub.com

Tip 43 – Handwritten Notes

In this age where people communicate by email or comments in social media, the art of giving handwritten notes is appreciated, especially by the older generation.

After meeting a potential client, hand out a note showing your appreciation for their attendance. Leaving a good impression will make you stand out in their minds.

Here are some tips on writing handwritten notes.

http://www.bluestemmarketing.com/2014/11/handwritten-notes-real-estate-marketing/

Join our insider Real Estate community, visit
www.proREclub.com

Tip 44 – Be Open To Suggestions

Homebuyers and sellers are good sources of suggestions on how to simplify the process. Listen and take note of these. These are tips that can upscale your services.

Listen for consistent problems or bottle neck areas in the home transaction. Other realtors are always trying to improve the "smoothness" of their business. Maybe they found a software or a process that makes their life easier and increases their profits. If you have a question, **ask**.

Tip 45 – After Hours Answering Service

One good way of providing 24x7 service for travelling clients is by having an after-hours answering service. This can be outsourced by hiring virtual sales agents or virtual assistants.

http://fitsmallbusiness.com/real-estate-virtual-assistant/

Join our insider Real Estate community, visit
www.proREclub.com

OLD SCHOOL MARKETING

Before internet was available, realtors used three basic strategies in getting sales:

- ☐ Direct mail
- ☐ Cold Calls
- ☐ Door Knocking

Although technology has its counterparts, these 'old school methods' can still be effective.

After all, the strategy is still the same – targeted marketing and lead conversion.

The next section discusses some "modernized" old-school methods that may be worth considering in your marketing plan.

Join our insider Real Estate community, visit
www.proREclub.com

Tip 46 - Pizza Box Advertising

Who doesn't love pizza? It's hot, delicious and delivered in minutes. It has become this generation's comfort food.

As a realtor, why not invest in an attractive logo and advertise your business on pizza boxes? Most people eat their pizza as a group around the box so this will help in brand recognition if you have an attractive logo or catchy phrase.

Join our insider Real Estate community, visit
www.proREclub.com

Tip 47 - Classified Ad Posting

There are very many online classified ads – Craigslist, Zillow, RealRentals, etc. – where you can post houses for sale. How can your ad stand out? First, go through other ads. If you were searching for a house, what information is missing? Always think from the customer's point of view.

Make sure your ad contains frequently searched keywords:

- Location
- Price
- Availability date
- Special features and services

If there is anything unique about the place, mention it. Some examples are a well-maintained garden, privacy and new furniture. If you have a video that could help sell the place, post it there.

Tip 48 - Local Raffles

Raffles are an innovative idea. For properties that have been stagnant in the market for some time, why not sell ticket to raffles? The winner gets the house. Sellers earn enough from the ticket sales.

You may want to read cases where these were successful.

http://www.nytimes.com/2008/09/25/garden/25raffle.html

Join our insider Real Estate community, visit
www.proREclub.com

Tip 49 - Door Hangers

Colorful and eye-catching messages in door hangers can be very effective in advertising your business. Stock photos of beautiful homes and gardens are available on the web and you can use easy-to-use graphic design tools like Canva.com to create these door hangers.

Unlike flyers that people easily ignore, door hangers are very visible and has its purpose (the other side can be a 'do not disturb' sign just like in hotels). Distribution by post is also very convenient.

A creative way to distribute your business card is to have a detachable portion in the lower portion of the door card. You can give these away during networking events.

Look at how Joshua Smith was able to close deals using this technique
http://fitsmallbusiness.com/real-estate-door-hangers/

Join our insider Real Estate community, visit
www.proREclub.com

Tip 50 - Every Door Direct Mail Service

Send your marketing materials (for example, flyers, letters) using the USPS marketing service. To avoid wastage, you can carefully select homes using information like age, income and household size.

You also have the flexibility of designing and printing your own materials or partnering with affiliates of USPS.

While your business is growing, your niche may also be changing. The "EDDM" mapping tool can be re-used to change your choice of mailing routes.

Join our insider Real Estate community, visit
www.proREclub.com

Tip 51 - Radio and TV Advertising

Although everyone is active on the internet, TV and radio are still effective ways of reaching your target market.

- Join talk shows where the topics are related to flipping homes, home makeover and home improvements.

- Grant interviews for travel and cooking shows that feature your city.

- Produce commercials.

- Have a radio show featuring Q&A sessions with real estate experts

Tip 52 - Promotional Materials

These are still very effective in getting your business recognized. Distribute these on your events.

☐ Bumper stickers with catchy messages advertising your business. These go on your car, laptop, water bottle, mug. This is instant free advertising during traffic.

☐ Distribute your flyers on places that are frequently visited by homeowners – like stores selling furniture, tools/hardware, kitchen appliances. They may be considering new properties that are not too costly to maintain.

☐ People don't throw away useful items like pens, post-it notes, keychain tags, memo pads and umbrellas. The longer they use it, the more they will be reminded of your business name.

Join our insider Real Estate community, visit
www.proREclub.com

Tip 53 - Logo Exposure

Decide on an eye-catching logo that represents your realty business. Aside from using in your online profiles for brand recognition, these can also be printed on your promotional materials.

You can design a logo yourself using Canva. Or hire a freelancer to do it for you.

Canva.com

Tip 54 - Business Cards

We still hand out our business cards, especially in face-to-face meetings. Make sure that your card has all the necessary information, including your photo, logo, website and email address.

Something about a business card means you are legit. Get some today.

Tip 55 - Direct Mail Advertising

Create real estate postcards with beautiful pictures of a home or even an inspiring quote convincing people to own their own home. Make it attractive enough to post in their refrigerators or work area.

Always offer something valuable – like sales guarantees, coupons/discounts on handyman services or a calendar with pictures of your local community.

Join our insider Real Estate community, visit
www.proREclub.com

Tip 56 – Stickers On Your Car

Post stickers on your car advertising your realtor services. While parking or on traffic, you are advertising for free.

Don't go overboard here. But if you can think of a catchy phrase that direct people to your website, then by all means add it to your car.

SOCIAL MEDIA MARKETING

Social media is fast becoming the focus of everyone's lives. At the start, the objective of social media was to build relationships with friends. But now, businesses have tapped the power of social media to reach their target markets.

In real estate marketing, there have been many strategies in using social media to further sales. But as with many tools, it would be wise assess the strengths and weaknesses of various social media options.

Join our insider Real Estate community, visit
www.proREclub.com

Tip 57 - Goal Setting

With so many social media sites available, you have to evaluate which is the most effective for your niche. Generally, the most frequently-used sites by realtors are:

- Facebook
- Twitter
- LinkedIn
- Instagram
- Snapchat
- YouTube

For your business, some questions you need to ask are:

1. Which sites do my target customers frequently use?

2. How much time can I spend to maintain my account?

3. Does it provide analytics? Although regular posting will build your SEO, you need to find out the times when your posts are frequently read, which posts are popular and what topics people are eager to know more about.

Block a regular time to build your social media profile and evaluate the effectivity of your posts. The eventual goal in using social media is to reach people within your niche and lead them to your website. Your website is the real 'showroom'.

Join our insider Real Estate community, visit
www.proREclub.com

Tip 58 - Scheduling

I love this quote below from Tom Greening:

"All time management begins with planning."

The best way to build your website's search engine ranking is by posting frequently in various social media sites – the most popular being Twitter, Facebook, Pinterest, Instagram and YouTube. Since your main activities are onsite (e.g. viewing properties, talking to clients and other brokers), how do you ensure that your online presence is active? The answer is Planning and Automation.

Maintain a content planner, which is a calendar of your social media activity. Write down blog topics, quotes, images, announcements, videos that you plan to post. It does not have to be daily, just maintain a regular schedule.

Automation is a productive way to release your social media posts on a fixed schedule and across different social media. Some popular apps are Hootsuite and Buffer. Just make sure that aside from their flexibility, they provide analytics so that you are informed about the engagement and reach of your posts. This will help you plan your future posts more effectively.

If there are fellow realtors or associations that you follow in Instagram or Facebook, drop a quick comment in

Join our insider Real Estate community, visit
www.proREclub.com

response to their post. All your social media accounts should have reference to your website. The idea is to point people to your website, which is a central place for you to showcase your services.

Join our insider Real Estate community, visit
www.proREclub.com

Tip 59 - LinkedIn

LinkedIn is highly recommended for realtors because of four reasons.

One, you can build your professional image. Once you have decided on your Personal Branding, the next step is to build an impressive profile in LinkedIn. Post a professional-looking photo of yourself, with a sincere smile. Prepare a readable yet concise biography to introduce yourself, the market you are passionately reaching out to and testimonials from satisfied clients. Also mention any credentials or awards to build your credibility as realtor.

Second, LinkedIn is a very powerful tool to build your own network of professionals in the real estate and other allied industries (like interior design, movers, etc.). If you are just starting out, you can build your basic network by allowing LinkedIn to scan contacts in your email. An invitation will be sent to them and once they agree, they will be your first level connection. Just like Facebook, LinkedIn continually searches for other professionals that match your profile and prompts you to connect. You can also browse "friends of friends". If you want to connect with them, you can request your first level connection to introduce you.

Third, you can search for industry professionals using keywords like their location, expertise or affiliations.

Join our insider Real Estate community, visit
www.proREclub.com

Fourth, LinkedIn is where you can post and share useful content to your network. You can also comment and share your thoughts on their content.

Tip 60 - YouTube

Posting content in your own YouTube channel will improve your search ranking in Google. It is the best platform to introduce yourself to your niche. You can post videos of the following:

- Background of experience and services
- Property listings
- Information
- Lectures
- Interviews
- E-book promotions
- Neighborhood activities
- Virtual tours

To maintain your ranking, posting has to be done on a regular basis. Always remember to include call-to-action links and share icons.

Vimeo is an alternative video platform.

Join our insider Real Estate community, visit
www.proREclub.com

Tip 61 – Facebook

Create a Facebook business page where you can post your profile and services. You are allowed to create tabs for "Featured Listings" or categories by area.

It is recommended to post videos and images since these have more visual impact. The same videos posted in your YouTube channel can also be posted in Facebook.

http://www.practicalecommerce.com/15-facebook-marketing-tips-for-realtors

For a fee, Facebook can expose your business page to FB members whose demographics match your niche. They also provide analytics – level of engagement and when the posts are being read.

Facebook also allows you to schedule when your posts will be released. All this becomes possible with a facebook business page. You must have one as a realtor.

Join our insider Real Estate community, visit
www.proREclub.com

Tip 62 – Twitter

Using the right keyword hashtags, you can use advanced search to target people on the lookout for properties in your city. If you use highly targeted keywords, you may be able to streamline the search to serious homebuyers.

Twitter also allows you to follow activities of market leaders and leave your comments. This will help improve your SEO.

Some simple re-tweets can make you looked plugged into your community and the real estate market.

Build a group of followers by also following their sites. Choose those with profiles interested in real estate. The crowd is here. Engage them with some fun topics, all within 140 characters.

Join our insider Real Estate community, visit
www.proREclub.com

Tip 63 – Livestream

One of the latest in social media is livestream videos, where invited guests can watch an event (like auctions, property viewings) without leaving their homes.

This can be one way of capturing leads. For those interested to get the latest insider information on a specific area, get their emails. Make it sound exclusive and for a short period of time only.

https://www.businessinsider.com.au/a-sydney-real-estate-agent-will-live-stream-the-auction-of-a-surry-hills-apartment-on-facebook-2016-4

Join our insider Real Estate community, visit
www.proREclub.com

Tip 64 – Keywords

Learn as much as you can about Google searches. Be updated with tips and tricks that you can readily use in building your business. Check out the Google keyword planner (its free). And type in searches you think people will type when looking for a realtor.

Match your content to these keywords. This is how people find you in the search engines. You may think folks type in just "realtors" when they are searching. But truthfully, they type like they think. For example: "Who is the best realtor near me." The results may surprise you. Start testing these things today.

Join our insider Real Estate community, visit
www.proREclub.com

WEBSITE OPTIMIZATION

In the online world, your website represents your business. If you want to make a good first impression, your website should look professional, clean and visually pleasing.

The next section will give you some tips to optimize your website so that it ranks high in search engine results, looks incredible and grows your business

There are two categories:

- ☐ Onsite SEO
- ☐ Offsite SEO

Your website should be available in mobile devices.

Join our insider Real Estate community, visit
www.proREclub.com

Tip 65 - Targeting Transients

You may meet people who may be staying in your city on a short-term basis.

For those assigned on long business trips, they may not want to stay in a hotel. Suggest homey apartments available for short-term lease. Given a bigger space, they can cook and invite friends, feeling right "at home".

For students on a budget, show them some dormitories or shared-space arrangements. Assure parents of the safety of the area.

The recently-divorced would also appreciate a quick transfer to a private, quiet place.

If you are a new realtor, work with these transient groups as a starting point. They can give you positive testimonials or be your source of referrals.

Create interest in your city by contributing articles to travel blogs. From a resident's point of view, you can feature seldom-known yet interesting places in your hometown.

Try sending the top-10 of the following:

- Restaurants
- Picnic spots
- Walking tours (for day visitors)
- Novelty shops and souvenirs
- Nature trips
- Historical landmarks

Make sure that each post has a link to your website and a short description of yourself and your business.

Someone reading the travel blog may actually be doing a web search prior to moving the city. Or someone following your top-10 tips may eventually decide to settle in the area – falling in love with your town and its people.

Tip 67 – Blog Posts With Value

Aim for short blog posts that are written in a friendly manner. Choose topics that address the needs, questions and concerns of buyers and sellers.

Some examples are:

- How to identify a profitable property investment
- Checklist in buying old properties
- Top 10 reasons why X city is the best place to raise a family
- The fastest way to sell your property

If it is full of valuable information, readers will keep your article as reference for themselves or share it with a friend looking for the same information.

Join our insider Real Estate community, visit
www.proREclub.com

Tip 68 – Source Articles Online

For a website to be optimized, there needs to be regular posting of well-written blogs. You may have many topics in mind but writing can be a challenge. Try content providers that specialize in real estate. For a fee, they can provide a fixed number of articles for your website.

Check out these websites:
Iwriter.com
Upwork.com
getwrittn.com

100
Join our insider Real Estate community, visit
www.proREclub.com

Tip 69 – Include MLS Listings

Through IDX (Internet Data Exchange), MLS listings can be made available in your website.

See the link for guidelines in using IDX:

https://placester.com/real-estate-marketing-academy/what-is-idx-explanation-beginner-agent/

Join our insider Real Estate community, visit
www.proREclub.com

Tip 70 – Watching Lead Statistics

If your website is on Wordpress or you have a Facebook page, check the statistics provided:

- ☐ How many read your posts and at what times in the day?
- ☐ Which posts created engagements or reactions?
- ☐ Which had an impact and how much response did you get?

Monitoring these statistics will help improve your posts. You will know the best times for your publishing posts and ads. It will also help you decide which topics you will delegate to content writers.

Join our insider Real Estate community, visit
www.proREclub.com

Tip 71 – Naming your website

It is recommended for your domain to be the same as your name so that your website will show first in organic searches. Choose the .com domain names which is still the most commonly used extension.

If you cannot use your name, choose one that can be easily remembered and is consistent with your branding.

Join our insider Real Estate community, visit
www.proREclub.com

Tip 72 – Testimonials

Feature three of your best written testimonials prominently on the first page of your website.

If you have video testimonials, these are more convincing since a real person is praising your services. You can show these videos with prospects to build your credibility.

Word-of-mouth is very powerful advertising.

Tip 73 – Blog Comments

Readers usually leave comments on controversial or emotional topics. Encourage them to share their own experiences. Ask open-ended questions to encourage discussion.

This will raise your rankings in social media.

Join our insider Real Estate community, visit
www.proREclub.com

Tip 74 – Link Building from Local Businesses

If other websites link to pages in your website, this increases the popularity of your site and pushes you higher in search engine ranking.

As related to tip# 17, you can request other local businesses to link to your website, either by promoting your business or sharing your blogs.

106
Join our insider Real Estate community, visit
www.proREclub.com

Tip 75 – Google Maps

Make sure that your business location is registered in google maps. This will ensure high ranking in google searches.

Similarly, use plugins showing a map of your location on your Contacts page.

Join our insider Real Estate community, visit
www.proREclub.com

Tip 76 – Website without Music

Keep your website simple. Playing background music may distract visitors from your message. It could also slow down the response time of your website.

Join our insider Real Estate community, visit
www.proREclub.com

Tip 77 – Web Design Updates

Just like fashion, web designs change frequently. Be observant when visiting other websites. Look out for improvements that can be applied to your website.

If you are not tech-savvy, this is one task that you can outsource to experts in web design. They keep up with trends in the industry and can give you options.

A redesign every three years is reasonable.

Join our insider Real Estate community, visit
www.proREclub.com

Tip 78 – Mortgage Calculator in Website

Include a mortgage calculator so that visitors to your website can conveniently compute their loan amortization.

There are other simple tools that a potential buyer might need on-hand like:

- ☐ Option to tag properties and write notes
- ☐ Online chatbox

As you apply SEO strategies, followers may be leaving comments in your website. Know the appropriate way to respond.

Urgent ones will need a phone number from you. However, minor and repetitive queries can be addressed by a FAQ page in your website or may be a good idea for a blog post.

I highly advise using an automatic follow up system. Check out realtorhammer.com. They have pre built follow ups built into their CRM. Huge time saver for your business.

111
Join our insider Real Estate community, visit
www.proREclub.com

Tip 80 – Video Posting to Website

An alternative to blogging is to post a video. You can use your YouTube videos to repurpose content

This has been proven to rank high in google since most people prefer watching to reading.

Join our insider Real Estate community, visit
www.proREclub.com

Tip 81 – Increase SEO links

Find creative ways to increase links to your website. You can outsource this task to freelancers:

☐ Visit social forums related to real estate. People may have raised questions which you have already answered through a blog post. Leave short comments and provide a link to your post.

☐ Request other websites to link to your website.   These could be travel blogs or those in your network of business partners.

☐ Include your website in neighborhood directories.

Join our insider Real Estate community, visit
www.proREclub.com

Tip 82 – Links to Neighborhood Pages

If other websites are linking to yours, this is called backlinks. This can increase the rank of your web page since it appears that your post is popular enough for other websites to be linking to yours. This can happen by writing posts that are so interesting or valuable that it encourages sharing to others.

Another way is to agree with other bloggers to cross-link to each other's websites. You can partner with neighborhood business to promote each other's blogs or guest-post on their websites. Everyone needs fresh content.

Tip 83 – Multiple Links Per Blog Post

On each blog post, have at least five links. Some examples are:

      ☐ Linking to related blog posts in your own website
      ☐ Linking to the websites of experts in your network
      ☐ Linking to your contact page
      ☐ Linking to your e-book download or amazon sales page
      ☐ Hyperlinking text or pictures

This will build your google ranking.

115
Join our insider Real Estate community, visit
www.proREclub.com

Tip 84 – Activation of web pages

If you don't have time to post a blog, you can still activate your website by refreshing older pages. Update your mission statement and 'About' pages. Add events or announcements. Categorize your blog posts.

Keep the content flowing, and when you build a team, have them do this for you.

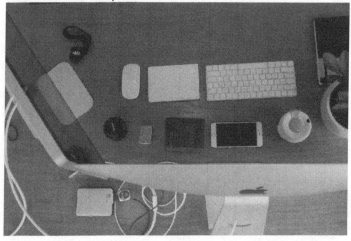

Join our insider Real Estate community, visit
www.proREclub.com

Tip 85 – Gain traffic through affiliates

Affiliates may not be in the business of real estate but they are paid to give you leads by promoting your website or e-book. This is one way to increase traffic to your website.

Join our insider Real Estate community, visit
www.proREclub.com

Tip 86 – Subscriptions

Your blog posts can be shared to anyone. Make sure that there is a subscribe button in your post. Anyone interested to receive regular newsletters can subscribe to your mailing list. You can offer a free digital product in exchange for their email address.

Join our insider Real Estate community, visit
www.proREclub.com

Tip 87 – Make an app

Identify unmet needs in the market that can be solved through a new app. Or you can identify the weak points and develop an improved version of the app.

You may get ideas from the following mobile apps available in IOS and Android:

- ☐ Mortgage calculator
- ☐ Sitegeist provides interesting data about an area like average age, temperature, commuting trends
- ☐ Vert is a conversion tool for size, weight, volume, length. Realtors need this readily available.
- ☐ Cam Scammer to scan documents directly from a mobile device. Realtors can send info to the office even while offsite.
- ☐ Dropbox to store documents in the cloud and therefore, available everywhere you are
- ☐ PDF Escape to keep a digital version of your signature. For documents while on the go, you can now add your signature to PDF documents

Outsource the building and testing of your app. Then use it for your business and freely share with fellow realtors to build its popularity.

Tip 88 – Live chat support

Enhance your website to include live chat. This is another task that can be outsourced so that your support can be available 24x7. You can capture emails and phone numbers using this tool. It's also one way to know the needs and concerns of your target market.

A very cool new tool being used is called Manychat.com which connects your website with your facebook messenger. Which you can set up to go right to your iphone.

Join our insider Real Estate community, visit
www.proREclub.com

Tip 89 – Own your website hosting

When you decide you need a website, make sure you own your server space. That way, you can make a custom email, add your own content anytime, and maintain control over your server space.

Smart business owners understand the importance of owning their server space.

A great provider is Bluehost.com, you can get started owning your own server space for around $4 dollars a month.

Check it out here:
http://www.bluehost.com/track/bigz014/

Join our insider Real Estate community, visit
www.proREclub.com

Tip 90 – Create a quick website yourself

You can now create your own website using Weebly and Wix. These were developed for people who don't code yet want a ready website in minutes. These have beautiful and professional-looking template websites where you can drag-and-drop features to slightly customize.

Link here:
https://www.weebly.com/
https://www.wix.com/
https://wordpress.com/

Join our insider Real Estate community, visit
www.proREclub.com

Tip 91 – Multiple Websites

If you are selling properties in different cities or towns, it would be a good idea to maintain multiple websites. You can customize your marketing strategies with this approach.

Join our insider Real Estate community, visit
www.proREclub.com

Tip 92 - Graphic Design

There are free graphic design tools like Canva which make it very easy to create presentations, Facebook covers, flyers, posters, invitations, etc.

See the link below:
https://www.canva.com/

Join our insider Real Estate community, visit
www.proREclub.com

Tip 93 – Support Advocacies

When your customers become your friends, they will be sharing their business or personal advocacies. Support them by posting on these topics. Or guest blogging on their websites.

Join our insider Real Estate community, visit
www.proREclub.com

Tip 94 – Ask the Expert Series

One good idea for a blog post or videos is to invite experts from your network – banker (mortgage adviser), home organizer, termite consultant.

It can be an interview/webinar where they give tips on homeowners' common concerns.   At the end, allow some Q&A where the audience can ask questions.

Tip 95 – Infographics

Infographics is information presented in graphic or visual form. For your realty business, you can present statistics and top-10 tips.

You can use infographics to create variety in your blog posts. These can also be given away as digital gifts to get leads or printed in door hangers, postcards, bookmarks or other promotional materials.

See the link below for inspiration:

https://www.jasonfox.me/60-real-estate-infographics-you-can-use-to-ignite-your-content-marketing/

Join our insider Real Estate community, visit
www.proREclub.com

Tip 96 - Newsletters

Email marketing is a popular and effective marketing tool to communicate with a captive market and build your SEO. Visitors to your website and social media accounts can "opt in" or agree to receive regular newsletters from you. In return for giving out their email, you give them a free gift (usually in digital form like an e-book, whitepaper, checklist, template or infographic).

Make sure that your emails provide valuable content so that people stay subscribed and share to their friends, who will in turn "opt in" also.

You can create multiple subscription types, targeting different market groups. For example, one email campaign can target retirees while another can target young families. This is more effective than generic emails since the newsletters can focus on their interests.

There are other ways to build your email list:
- Create a Twitter campaign to promote an e-book. Require an email address to redeem.

- Publish links to your landing page through LinkedIn discussion groups or real estate forums. Your landing page will require input of an email address to redeem the gift.

- Your YouTube channel should have a link to your landing page, especially on the instructional

Join our insider Real Estate community, visit
www.proREclub.com

videos. People who want to learn more want to be alerted on the latest.

- If you are teaching online, include a link in your profile where students can click to the landing page.

- Promote offers through your Google+ Page "About" Section.

- In your guest blogs, include a call-to-action link that leads to your landing page.

- Work with your affiliates or partners to run a promotion on their websites or webinars.

- From visitors to open houses or trade shows, collect email addresses and don't forget to send a welcome email to confirm their opting-in to your list.

- From your city meetups or other networking activities, collect their email addresses through online registration.

- If you are sending promotional materials through direct mail, ask prospects if they want to be reached through newsletters instead in exchange for a free online gift.

Join our insider Real Estate community, visit
www.proREclub.com

- In your paid ads, always add a link to your landing page.

For your newsletter, check out the automatic CRM for realtors at realtorhammer.com

130
Join our insider Real Estate community, visit
www.proREclub.com

Tip 97 – E-Book Marketing

This generation has turned to e-books because it can read easily from mobile devices. Secondly, e-books are short and direct.

If you have posted a lot of blogs discussing the same topic, you can repurpose content by putting these all together into an e-book. This can be sold in amazon or given away for free in your marketing campaigns.

How do you promote an e-book? Aside from the usual way of sharing in social media, you can use these:

☐ Create interest by posting a portion of the e-book. Use LinkedIn Slideshare.

☐ Hire a voice actor from Fiverr (or a friend with a good speaking voice) to read the entire e-book and transform this to audio books.

☐ Summarize the major points and create an infographic. This can be another digital gift.

☐ Create a webinar or online course based on the major topics of the e-book.

☐ Create "quotes" from the e-book and post in Twitter and Instagram.

Join our insider Real Estate community, visit
www.proREclub.com

☐ Promote the e-book in your newsletters.

☐ Print copies for distribution in events.
Request an industry expert or market leader to comment on the e-book.

☐ Get testimonials from readers.

E-books can also be sold as books. Have some available for giveaway in events.

132
Join our insider Real Estate community, visit
www.proREclub.com

Tip 98 - Paid Advertising

If you are restricted by a low advertising budget, check for local websites selling ad space. Although they may not have a large readership, doing so will already build your online presence.

Another are one-time websites created to get sponsors for school activities. These are very affordable. Aside from helping the kids, your SEO exposure will improve.

Google Adwords, Bing and Yahoo Ads

Signing up for these services are absolutely free. The advertising fees, however, will depend on your keyword quality score (popularity of keywords based on statistics gathered from searches) and bid (volume of buyers for that keyword).

Both have the following features:

☐ Pay-per-click (PPC) wherein you pay only when someone clicks on your ad.
☐ Option to set up an advertising budget
☐ Targeted advertising based on location, times & day of week, demographics
☐ Analytics. Feedback on the performance of your ad

Join our insider Real Estate community, visit
www.proREclub.com

What makes them different? Google is the more popular choice for searches. Bing, however, has a lower cost-per-click than Google and will give you a higher ad position.

Tip 98 – Online Marketplaces

Zillow.com

Aside from LinkedIn, this is a real-estate website that you must join. It links local realtors (as well as other professionals like builders, photographers and property managers) to people who want to rent, buy or sell homes. What makes the site stand out is that clients can customize their search of local realtors based on their needs. If they need someone specializing in foreclosures or relocation, they can search accordingly.

Registration is free and easy. Similar to LinkedIn, you will need to create an attractive profile. If you have any specialties, highlight these. Always add links to your website and active social media accounts.

Promote yourself by listing down all your past sales. Also add positive testimonials from previous clients.

Lastly, start linking the properties you are handling.

Setting up your profile will only take a few hours but your exposure through Zillow is definitely worth your time. Keep your profile active by continually adding testimonials, sales and property listings.

Realtor.com

This website is also a popular home search tool. If you are a member of the National Association of Realtors (NAR), you should seriously consider registering your profile.

This site is intended for properties under Multiple Listing Services (MLS), with updates every 15 minutes. Therefore, everyone gets the latest availability status.

It provides very user-friendly information on the community, which is a big plus for people who are considering relocating to a city. Details like local school ratings, climate, cost of living, employment opportunities, demographics (age distribution, marital status, household income and educational background) and crime index are available in the site.

Another big advantage is its availability on mobile devices. So you get the latest information even while offsite.

Join our insider Real Estate community, visit
www.proREclub.com

Redfin.com Partnership

Redfin is now called the Amazon counterpart in real estate. It goes beyond home searches. It is a one-stop shop that assists customers end-to-end, from house hunting to getting that loan. They profile customers and customize their services. Listings include virtual tours and a wide search criteria of realtors as well as home-related services and vendors.

You have the option to join Redfin as one of its brokers. Or if you prefer to work independently, you can join as its partner. If Redfin agents have clients with very specific requirements not within their scope (like a specific budget or area), they can refer these to you. As a local realtor, you are in a better position to have these property listings.

Join our insider Real Estate community, visit
www.proREclub.com

Movoto.com

Movoto gives valuable assistance to real estate agents by letting them focus on meeting the needs of their clients. Realtors no longer have to worry about getting leads, pre-screening clients, working on the legalities. Using technology, Movoto matches home buyers/sellers with their ideal realtor.

MLS Listings

Browse through homes available for sale in MLS. Search for those with high potential and promote yourself as a realtor in the area. Make sure that you leave a link to your website.

Trulia.com

Register as a realtor in Trulia. Property sellers will contact you once they see your profile. Also join their community forums to leave comments and suggestions.

Tip 99 – Landing Pages

The objective behind landing pages is to capture the names and emails of prospective clients. In all your social media accounts and web pages, make sure that there is a link leading to a landing page. In exchange for this, promise a digital product or promotional item.

Click the link below for step-by-step guide to creating a landing page that converts visitors into leads:

https://placester.com/real-estate-marketing-academy/video-marketing-academy-secrets-22-use-landing-pages-convert-visitors-leads/?utm_source=fitsmallbusiness&utm_campaign=fsb-traffic-2017&utm_medium=academy

Join our insider Real Estate community, visit
www.proREclub.com

Tip 100 – Google Searches

If you don't have a property listing for a serious homebuyer, take the initiative to search through Google "We buy houses" and the city. You can co-broke with other realtors.

Look through the free online tool called Google Adwords Keyword planner. You can see what people are searching for and buy ads for those terms. So when someone searches "realtor in spring texas" your name will appear.

Join our insider Real Estate community, visit
www.proREclub.com

Tip 101 – Autoresponders

When you are working with many clients simultaneously, make use of auto responder series to send the appropriate emails based on the progress of the transaction. The objective is to make them feel that you are their sole client, so they get regular, customized messages from you.

See the link below:
https://www.marketingsherpa.com/article/case-study/5-strategies2

One of the simplest and relator specific auto responders is realtorhammer.com. This tool has pre built follow ups that you can install right into your CRM. This means that when someone signs up to your newsletter, or when you add prospects to your list, you can drip email them at a certain pace, and have the funnel respond based on your criteria. Its pretty amazing.

Check it out today at: www.realtorhammer.com

Join our insider Real Estate community, visit
www.proREclub.com

Tip 102 - Communication tools

With everybody glued to their mobile phones, make sure that your website is mobile-friendly. Include links to communication tools like Skype, Zoom or Gotomeeting to make yourself readily available to motivated buyers and sellers. Remember that potential clients may be living anywhere in the world so you need to be reachable across time zones.

In Facebook, turn on notifications so that you don't miss any message. Compose automatic messages in facebook messenger to assure clients that their message was received and will be addressed soon.

For quick face-to-face meetings, take advantage of Zoom or Gotomeeting. The next best thing to meeting personally is a video call with clients and industry partners. Clarifications and decisions can be made faster.

Remember, "the early bird catches the worm", so it pays to be the first to respond.

Join our insider Real Estate community, visit
www.proREclub.com

Thanks for reading this book and expanding your mind to the possibilities to growing your real estate business. For insider videos, tips and tools to grow your business, visit proreclub.com

Additional Resources

To see a list of all the links, resources and helpful articles from this book...

Visit www.proREclub.com/Resources

Join our insider Real Estate community, visit
www.proREclub.com

Made in the USA
San Bernardino, CA
26 December 2018